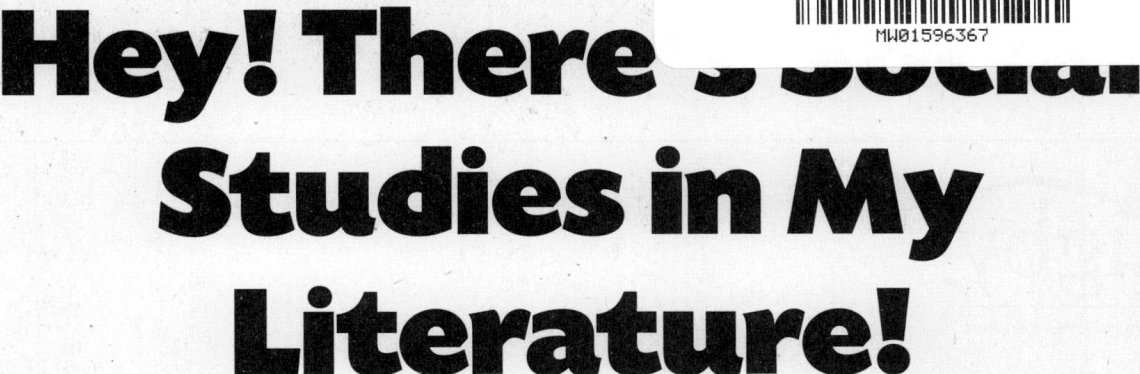

Hey! There's Social Studies in My Literature!

Using Literature to Support Social Studies Standards

Justine Dunn

Illustrated by Becky Radtke

Rigby®

A Harcourt Achieve Imprint

Dedications and Acknowledgments

I would like to dedicate this book to my baby angel, Shaelin Rae, and to my loving husband, Ray.

–Justine Dunn

A Harcourt Achieve Imprint

Production
DogTrick Studios

Production Coordinator
Perla Arce-Franke

Cover Illustrator
Aaron Romo

Interior Illustrator
Becky Radtke

The Trip Back Home, illustration copyright ©2000 by Bo Jia, used with permission of Harcourt, Inc.

ISBN-13: 978-1-4190-3400-8
ISBN-10:   1-4190-3400-6

Printed in the United States of America.
1 2 3 4 5 6 7 8 9 862 10 09 08 07 06

TABLE OF CONTENTS

Rigby Best Teachers Press
Hey! There's Social Studies... SV 9781419034008

Introduction

Literacy is often solely associated with reading; however, literacy *should* and *can* be taught throughout the school day and across the curriculum. *Hey! There's Social Studies in My Literature!* is designed to help teachers combine quality children's literature with hands-on social studies activities. There is a wealth of quality children's literature that supports the connection between social studies and literacy. This resource provides suggestions for read-alouds and coordinating activities for teaching basic social studies skills, which are correlated to the National Social Studies Standards. The activities can also be used with other children's books or on their own. The Suggested Social Studies Literature List on pages 91–92 can help you incorporate social studies into your classroom library.

There is an inextricable linking of family, culture, and community in the teaching and learning of social studies. The evolution of each child's social understandings about the world begins with self and family, expanding to the child care and educational setting. In developing these social inquiries, teachers first focus on what children know and are able to do. Then they help children scaffold additional learning to elaborate their understandings of the world around them. A sensitive, respectful approach to child and family sets the tone for each child's broader social learning experience.

(Mindes, 2005)

NCSS defines social studies as "the integrated study of the social sciences and humanities to promote civic competence." Within the school program, social studies provides coordinated, systematic study drawing upon such disciplines as anthropology, archaeology, economics, geography, history, law, philosophy, political science, psychology, religion, and sociology, as well as appropriate content from the humanities, mathematics, and natural sciences.

(National Council for the Social Studies, NCSS)

Each literature selection will be accompanied by the following:

National Social Studies Standards

The National Social Studies Education Standards can be found on the Internet at http://www.socialstudies.org/standards/strands/. It is important to become familiar with these standards as well as your district's standards and curriculum, as they should be used for instructional planning. In most schools, the teacher is able to decide how best to deliver instruction that meets the objectives set forth in the standards. Teachers should consider their own teaching style when creating activity plans based on standards. Because standards and benchmarks are crucial for educators today, each activity notes the specific standard(s) and skill(s) being addressed.

Social Studies Vocabulary

Students should be familiar with social studies vocabulary so they can comprehend and discuss concepts. You will find a list of suggested social studies vocabulary words in each unit and on page 90. Post these words in your Social Studies Center, around the room, or on a social studies bulletin board. Model how these words are used when discussing social studies concepts and encourage children to use these vocabulary words when they talk about social studies. Write the appropriate social studies vocabulary words on sentence strips and review the words before each unit.

Prereading Activity

The value of preparing students for reading has been recognized in professional literature since the turn of the twentieth century. Research continues to support the practice of preparing students for reading and learning. (Readence, et. al., 2000) The *Prereading Activity* for each unit will help prepare the children and help you assess their background knowledge.

 ## Read-Aloud Activity

The *Read-Aloud Activities* in this book are whole-group activities that integrate literacy and social studies. Reading aloud introduces children to quality literature in a pleasing and comfortable format. Read the featured children's book aloud and work with children to help them complete the corresponding *Application and Practice Activity* and the *Extension Activity*.

 ## Application and Practice Activity

"Practice makes perfect" sums up the necessity for children to use what they are learning. When possible, provide opportunities that allow children to use what they are learning in context rather than in isolation. For example, the *Application and Practice Activity* immediately follows the *Read-Aloud Activity*.

 ## Extension Activity

Because children enter your room with many different academic levels, instruction should be modified to meet individual needs. The *Extension Activity* is a more challenging one. If children master the *Application and Practice Activity*, the *Extension Activity* can be used to extend learning to a higher level.

Literacy Center Ideas

Literacy Centers provide a wide variety of learning opportunities for children. You can foster children's scientific development by providing environments rich in language, where thinking is encouraged, uniqueness is valued, and exploration is supported. Suggestions for activities in the following Literacy Centers are listed for each literature selection.

 **Reading/Writing**    **Art**

 **Math**    **Dramatic Play**

 **Science**    **Kids in the Kitchen**

 **Social Studies**

 <u>Caution:</u> *Some activities include using edible items. Always check for food sensitivities and allergies before serving food or allowing children to handle food.*

Before each activity is presented, gather your children in a whole group to discuss and demonstrate appropriate behavior and procedures for Literacy Centers. Ask the children to help create guidelines for participating in the Literacy Centers and ask for volunteers to help demonstrate proper use of the materials in each center.

Rigby Best Teachers Press
Hey! There's Social Studies... SV 9781419034008

Five Minute Social Studies Fun

Reinforcing concepts and skills can be accomplished in many ways. It is important to keep things interesting for your children. Too much practice on the same material in the same way can lead to boredom or frustration. *Five Minute Social Studies Fun* is a quick whole-group reinforcement of the concepts and skills being addressed. It can also be used as an informal assessment.

Home Connection

Children learn best when they are interested and excited about what they are doing. Their interest and excitement don't have to end when they leave your classroom. One of the most important factors that can lead to a successful program is parental involvement. Not only can parents support your instructional efforts, they can also reinforce and reemphasize the strategies you share with children.

Send home the parent letter located in each unit in order to reinforce what you are doing in the classroom. All of the home activities in this book can be done during a child's daily routines. They require no special equipment or detailed planning. Parents can use them to do something pleasant with their child, add some interest to an otherwise routine activity, or keep their children interested or occupied.

Send home the *Supply Request Letter* on page 89 the week prior to each unit. Parents are a wonderful resource and enjoy contributing to the classroom.

Scope and Sequence

Title	Social Studies Skills	Social Studies Standard	Page Numbers
Apple Pie 4th of July	There are various aspects of culture that allow people to live and work together, and cultural differences are expressions of an individual's unique cultural heritage.	Culture	10–17
Families Are Different	Families can be made up of many different people in many different combinations.	Individual Development and Identity	18–26
Me on the Map	Mapping skills develop from the ability to imagine relationships between and among places.	People, Places, and Environments	27–33
The First Thing My Mama Told Me	Personal identity is shaped by many factors, including culture, family, and friends.	Individual Development and Identity	34–41
Check It Out! The Book About Libraries	Institutions are created to help carry out the social values and goals of the community.	Individuals, Groups, and Institutions	42–49
The Trip Back Home	Culture has an impact on our lives by giving unique individuals a common set of beliefs, knowledge, values, and traditions.	Culture	50–57
Worksong	Basic economic concepts such as production, consumption, and interdependence are affected by community workers, businesses in a neighborhood, and resources of states and nations.	Production, Distribution, and Consumption	58–64
The Computer	Science and technology influence personal lives as well as societal actions and values.	Science, Technology, and Society	65–71
A River Ran Wild	The survival of our planet depends on both an exchange of information and mutual cooperation.	Global Connections	72–80
Good Citizenship Counts	Citizenship obligations and skills are learned and practiced not only in the classroom but also in a variety of settings.	Civic Ideals and Practices	81–88

Wong, Janet S. (2002). *Apple Pie 4th of July*. San Diego: Harcourt, Inc.

 ## National Social Studies Standard: Culture

"Human beings create, learn, and adapt culture. Culture helps us to understand ourselves as both individuals and members of various groups."

—National Council for the Social Studies

Social studies programs should include experiences that provide for the study of culture and cultural diversity, so that the learner can—

- explore and describe similarities and differences in the ways groups, societies, and cultures address similar human needs and concerns.

- give examples and describe the importance of cultural unity and diversity within and across groups.

 ## Social Studies Vocabulary

culture	tradition	nationality	holiday
differences	diversity	similarities	

 **Prereading Activity**

• **Materials:** *Apple Pie 4th of July* by Janet S. Wong

Look at the cover of the book with the children. Read the title together. Ask the children what they think this book might be about, and why they think so. Take a book walk to preview the text and illustrations. Discuss the word *nationality* with the children, and ask what nationality they think this family is. If children are aware of their own nationalities, ask them to share with the class.

 **Read-Aloud Activity**

• **Materials:** *Apple Pie 4th of July* by Janet S. Wong

Read the book *Apple Pie 4th of July* aloud with the children. Discuss the people on each page. Ask questions such as "What do their facial expressions tell you?" "Are these people of the same nationality or of different nationalities?" Ask children to name some things that are part of this family's *culture*.

 **Application and Practice Activity**

• **Materials:** chart paper, marker

Discuss the importance of one's culture with the children. Explain that culture is a way of life, and each family's culture is different. It is important to understand cultural diversity and accept that there are *similarities* and *differences* among cultures. Sharing information about your culture can help you to understand the culture of others. Ask children to share a sentence about something they do during a celebration in their family. It can be a holiday, a special meal, or a visit from a relative. Write children's responses on chart paper and discuss the uniqueness of each *tradition*.

Extension Activity

- **Materials:** books about culture (refer to the Suggested Social Studies Literature List on pages 91–92)

Allow children time to look through several books about different cultures. Ask them to find three things they did not know about that culture and share those things with the class.

Literacy Center Ideas

Reading/Writing: Family Menus

- **Materials:** paper, pencils, crayons or markers

Children can make a family menu and include items their family often eats. Encourage children to draw pictures and, if they are able, to write words on their menus. The children can save their menus and use them in the dramatic play area.

Math: Culture Counting

- **Materials:** Culture Counting activity (page 17), pencils, crayons

Make one copy of the Culture Counting activity for each child. Explain to children that they will be looking for items that represent different cultures. The children can color the items as they find them and count the number of each item. There are one piñata, two necklaces, three cakes, four menorahs, and five sets of chopsticks.

www.harcourtschoolsupply.com

12

Rigby Best Teachers Press
Hey! There's Social Studies... SV 9781419034008

Science: No More Brown Apples!

- **Materials:** one apple for every two children, knife, lemons, paper, pencils, chalkboard or dry erase board, chalk or dry erase marker

Write the words *Lemon* and *No Lemon* on the board. Children will have a partner for this experiment. One partner will write "Lemon" on a sheet of paper, and the other partner will write "No Lemon" on a separate sheet of paper. Cut each apple into quarters. Roll the lemons on a hard surface and cut each one in half. Then put the knife out of the children's reach. Ask the children to put two apple quarters on the paper labeled "Lemon" and two apple quarters on the paper labeled "No Lemon." Then have the children take one lemon half and squeeze it, cut side down, over the apple quarters on the paper labeled "Lemon." After a few hours, ask the children to observe the apple quarters and discuss the results.

Social Studies: Happy Holidays!

- **Materials:** an Internet-capable computer

Demonstrate for the children how to conduct an Internet search for holidays around the world. A Web site you can encourage them to visit is http://www.ncsu.edu/midlink/dec98/hol98.html. Ask children to find some holiday celebrations that are both similar to and different from their own holiday celebrations.

Art: Apple Prints

- **Materials:** one apple for every two children, knife, paper plates, newspaper, tempera paints, paper

Prior to the lesson, cover the work area with newspaper and pour several different colors of paint onto paper plates. Cut each apple in half and put the knife out of the children's reach. Model how to dip the apple half into the paint and press it onto the paper to make an apple print. Encourage the children to make several different prints using various colors. Remind the children that they will use each apple half in only one color so as not to mix them.

Dramatic Play: May I Take Your Order?

- **Materials:** small table and chairs, menus from the Reading/Writing activity on page 12, notepads, pencils, play dishes, apron

Using the menus from the Reading/Writing activity, children can pretend they are in a restaurant. They can order selections from other children's family menus.

 ## Kids in the Kitchen: Sharing Snack

- **Materials:** favorite foods from the children's families, paper plates, napkins, utensils

 *Caution: This activity uses edible items. Always check for food sensitivities and allergies before serving food or allowing children to handle food.*

Send home the Supply Request Letter on page 89 a few days before doing this activity. Ask families to send one favorite food that can be stored and served at room temperature to school with each child. Families should send enough to share with everyone. Ask children to wash their hands prior to the activity. Distribute a small sample of each food to the children. Ask the children to tell what food they brought and why it is one of their favorites. Allow children to sample the foods if they choose.

 ## Five Minute Social Studies Fun: Family Tree

- **Materials:** green and brown construction paper, crayons or markers

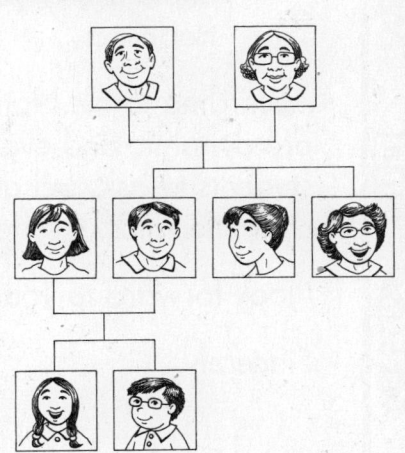

Children can make a simple family tree out of construction paper. They can use crayons or markers to draw each family member on the tree. If children are able, encourage them to write the names of the family members as well. You may want to include these family trees on a "Family Forest" bulletin board display.

 ## Home Connection

Copy the Parent Letter on page 16 and send it home the week you are conducting this unit.

Hey! There's Social Studies... SV 9781419034008

Date: _____

Dear Parents:

This week in social studies, we are learning about culture. We read the book *Apple Pie 4th of July* by Janet S. Wong and talked about cultural diversity. We created family menus and used them in the dramatic play area to take orders in a restaurant. We also made a sharing snack.

You can help your child appreciate cultural diversity by observing and discussing cultures that are different from your own. Here are some suggestions:

- Visit a local cultural center with your child. Ask questions of the guides at the center.

- Ask neighbors and friends to discuss their cultures with you and your child. Allow your child to ask questions.

- Discuss your own culture and traditions with your child. Explain why your family believes in and practices these traditions.

According to the National Council for the Social Studies, "Cultures are dynamic and ever-changing. The study of culture prepares students to ask and answer questions such as: What are the common characteristics of different cultures?"

I look forward to your participation in our learning experiences.

Sincerely,

Hey! There's Social Studies... SV 9781419034008

Name _____

Culture Counting

_____ cakes    _____ necklaces

_____ piñatas    _____ chopsticks

_____ menorahs

Rigby Best Teachers Press
Hey! There's Social Studies... SV 9781419034008

Families Are Different

by Nina Pellegrini

Pellegrini, Nina. (1991). *Families Are Different.*
New York: Holiday House.

National Social Studies Education Standard: Individual Development and Identity

"Given the nature of individual development and our own cultural context, students need to be aware of the processes of learning, growth, and development at every level of their school experience."

—National Council for the Social Studies

Social studies programs should include experiences that provide for the study of individual development and identity, so that the learner can—

- describe the unique features of one's nuclear and extended families.

- describe personal connections to place—especially place as associated with immediate surroundings.

Social Studies Vocabulary

family	mother	father	sister
brother	adopted	married	divorced
grandmother	grandfather	stepmother	stepfather

Prereading Activity

- **Materials:** *Families Are Different* by Nina Pellegrini, chart paper, white construction paper, crayons or markers

Ask children to discuss the members of their *family*. Tell children to think of the people in their family who live with them. Demonstrate how to make a Family Web. Draw a circle in the center of the chart paper and label it "me." Draw circles connected by lines to the center circle and insert drawings or names of other family members. Ask children to create their own family webs by drawing a picture of themselves in the center circle of the web and pictures of their family members in the other circles. If children are able, ask them to label their family web.

Read-Aloud Activity

- **Materials:** *Families Are Different* by Nina Pellegrini

Read the title of the story with the children. Ask children to share their family webs. Then read the story with the children. Discuss the similarities and differences between the families in the story and the families of the children in the class.

Application and Practice Activity

- **Materials:** several pictures of men, women, boys, and girls, all of varying ages and ethnicities

Discuss family name vocabulary with the children, such as *mother, father, sister, brother,* and so on. As you show the children each picture, ask them to suggest some possible family names for each person. For example, possible names for a picture of a man might be *father, brother, husband, uncle,* and *son*.

Extension Activity

- **Materials:** poster board, marker

Ask children to brainstorm a list of ways families are alike and different. Record these on a two-column chart titled "How Are Families Alike?" and "How Are Families Different?"

Literacy Center Ideas

Reading/Writing: Families Help

- **Materials:** paper, crayons or markers, pencils

Invite children to think about ways people in their family help one another. Ask children to draw pictures to show an example of helping in their family. Then have children write a simple sentence about their picture.

Math: Family Graph

- **Materials:** poster board, markers, self-stick notes

Prior to the activity, create a Family Graph on the poster board. Ask children to use markers to draw each of their family members on a self-stick note. Explain to children that they will be graphing just the family members that live with them. Then have children put each self-stick note in the proper category on the graph, such as mother, father, and so on. Children can count the total number of family members by category.

Rigby Best Teachers Press
Hey! There's Social Studies... SV 9781419034008

Science: Animal Families

- **Materials:** Animal Family Names activity (page 25), crayons or markers

Make a copy of the Animal Family Names activity for each child. The children can draw a picture of each animal in the space provided and read about animal family names.

Social Studies: Family Photo Album

- **Materials:** children's family photos, clear envelopes, double-sided tape, construction paper, three-hole paper punch, three book rings per child

One week prior to the activity, send home the Supply Request Letter on page 89. Ask parents to send at least five family photos to school with their child. The children can use double-sided tape to affix the clear envelopes on construction paper. Then they can insert their family photos in the envelopes. Encourage children to write captions or sentences for their pictures. After the children have completed their pages, punch holes in their papers and connect them with book rings. The children will enjoy sharing and looking through their family photo albums.

Rigby Best Teachers Press
Hey! There's Social Studies... SV 9781419034008

 ## Art: Family Puppets

- **Materials:** People Patterns (page 26); craft sticks; scissors; crayons or markers; glue or paste; brown, yellow, red, black, and gray yarn

Make several copies of the People Patterns prior to the activity. Children may need to use more than one pattern page. Ask children to think about the members of their family who live with them. Children can use crayons or markers to create a puppet of each family member, and they can use yarn for hair. Then have children cut out their puppets and attach them to craft sticks using glue or paste. Children can use their puppets in the dramatic play area.

 ## Dramatic Play: Family Fun

- **Materials:** puppets from the Art activity above, a table or something comparable children can use to hide behind for a puppet show, a large tablecloth

Prior to the activity, set up the dramatic play area for a puppet show. Drape a large tablecloth over a small table or something comparable. Children can use their family puppets to perform a puppet show for the class.

 ## Kids in the Kitchen: Family Fruit Salad

- **Materials:** fruit donated by each family (fresh or canned), cinnamon, plastic knives, large bowl, cutting board, strainer, large wooden or plastic spoon, one small bowl or tasting cup and one plastic spoon per child

 *Caution: This activity uses edible items. Always check for food sensitivities and allergies before serving food or allowing children to handle food.*

Send home the Supply Request Letter on page 89 a few days before doing this activity. Ask each family to send one type of fruit (fresh or canned) to school with their child. Ask children to wash their hands prior to the activity. Children can take turns cutting up their fruit or straining it if needed and adding it into the bowl. Add a sprinkle of cinnamon to the fruit salad and stir. Discuss the importance of family as children enjoy the snack.

 ## Five Minute Social Studies Fun: Family Poetry

- **Materials:** paper, pencils

Ask children to write a short poem about their family. Remind children that not all poems have to rhyme. Children can share their poems with the class if they choose.

 ## Home Connection

Copy the Parent Letter on page 24 and send it home the week you are conducting this unit.

Date:

Dear Parents:

This week in social studies, we are learning about families. We read the book *Families Are Different* by Nina Pellegrini and talked about different types of families.

You can help your child understand how families are different by discussing families and family members. Here are some suggestions:

- As you and your child read books or watch TV together, look for pictures that show families. Encourage your child to talk about the families and tell ways they are alike and different from your own family.

- Encourage your child to write a letter or draw a picture to send to a family member. Ask that family member to write back to your child.

- Together with your child, make a family tree. Discuss your family members and how they are related.

According to the National Council for the Social Studies, "In the early grades,...observing brothers, sisters, and older adults; looking at family photo albums; remembering past achievements and projecting oneself into the future...are appropriate activities because young learners develop their personal identities in the context of families, peers, schools, and communities."

Thank you for your participation.

Sincerely,

Rigby Best Teachers Press
Hey! There's Social Studies... SV 9781419034008

Name _____

Animal Family Names

Picture	Animal	Family Name
	deer	herd
	lion	pride
	elephant	herd
	chicken	flock
	fish	school
	giraffe	herd
	frog	army

Rigby Best Teachers Press
Hey! There's Social Studies... SV 9781419034008

People Patterns

Hey! There's Social Studies... SV 9781419034008

Me on the Map

by Joan Sweeney

Sweeney, Joan. (1996). *Me on the Map.*
New York: Crown Publishers, Inc.

National Social Studies Education Standard: People, Places, and Environments

"Technological advances connect students at all levels to the world beyond their personal locations. The study of people, places, and human-environment interactions assists learners as they create their spatial views and geographic perspectives of the world."

—National Council for the Social Studies

Social studies programs should include experiences that provide for the study of people, places, and environments, so that the learner can—

- construct and use mental maps of locales, regions, and the world that demonstrate understanding of relative location, direction, size, and shape.

- interpret, use, and distinguish various representations of the earth, such as maps, globes, and photographs.

- use appropriate resources, data sources, and geographic tools such as atlases, data bases, grid systems, charts, graphs, and maps to generate, manipulate, and interpret information.

 ## Social Studies Vocabulary

map	street	town	state
country	bodies of water	world	landmarks

 ## Prereading Activity

- **Materials:** *Me on the Map* by Joan Sweeney, maps, globe

Invite children to look at a globe and some maps. Explain that maps and globes are tools that can be used to locate places on Earth. Take a picture walk through the book with the children. Ask children to discuss the illustrations and compare them to the globe and maps that are in the classroom.

 ## Read-Aloud Activity

- **Materials:** *Me on the Map* by Joan Sweeney

Read the book aloud with the children. Point out that the story begins and ends with the girl in her room. Discuss the maps in the book and draw children's attention to the features on each map.

 ## Application and Practice Activity

- **Materials:** one large white sheet of construction paper per child, crayons or markers

Ask children to think about their rooms. Discuss the layout of a room, where things are located, and important features such as doorways and windows. Children can use crayons or markers to make a map of their room. Encourage children to look at the map of the girl's room in the story for reference.

Rigby Best Teachers Press
Hey! There's Social Studies... SV 9781419034008

Extension Activity

- **Materials:** maps, large index cards, marker

To help children remember directions, explain an acronym for north, south, east, and west. Refer to these directions on a compass rose and tell children that they can remember the directions by using the phrase "**N**ever **E**at **S**our **W**atermelon." Make sure the children understand that they have to start at the top of the compass rose and go to the right, or clockwise, when saying this phrase. Write the letters *N*, *E*, *S*, and *W* on large index cards and put them on the appropriate walls in your classroom.

Literacy Center Ideas

Reading/Writing: I Can Read a Map!

- **Materials:** I Can Read a Map! activity (page 33), math counters for each child

Make a copy of the I Can Read a Map! activity for each child and provide each child with several math counters. Children can look for words they know on the activity page. Then have children put a math counter on each word they know.

Math: Map Puzzles

- **Materials:** maps of your community, your state, and your country

Prior to the activity, cut the maps into several large pieces, based on the children's abilities. Write the name of the map on the back of each piece so they can easily be sorted if they are mixed up. Put the pieces in large plastic zipper bags and label the bags with the name of each map. The children can count how many pieces are in each bag, put the map together, and count the number of cities, roads, states, rivers, and so on.

 ## Science: Science on a Map?

- **Materials:** an Internet-capable computer

Show the children how to log on to http://www.weather.com/ to look at some weather maps. Explain to the children that they can find science on a map by looking at weather maps. They can explore current temperatures, weather warnings, and forecasts for their area as well as other areas in the world.

 ## Social Studies: Globe Game

- **Materials:** globe

The children can play a globe game by gently spinning a globe and putting their finger on it to stop it. Wherever their finger lands, help the children read the name of the location on the globe.

 ## Art: It's All in the Name

- **Materials:** construction paper, crayons or markers

Explain to children that people often name special landmarks and bodies of water based on the way they look. Children can draw maps that include landmarks or bodies of water. Then children can name their landmarks and bodies of water according to how they look, such as "Snake River" or "Rainbow Arch."

 ## Dramatic Play: In the Neighborhood

- **Materials:** miniature houses, buildings, cars, and people; blocks; paper; crayons or markers

Children can use the blocks to "build" a neighborhood, including streets. Then children can use miniature houses, buildings, cars, and people to complete the neighborhood. Have children name the streets and buildings and draw a simple map of the neighborhood they created.

 ## Kids in the Kitchen: Munchable Map Toast

- **Materials:** place mats, one slice of bread per child, plastic knives, butter or margarine, small plastic or paper cups, milk, food coloring, paintbrushes, toaster

 _Caution:_ *This activity uses edible items. Always check for food sensitivities and allergies before serving food or allowing children to handle food.*

Prior to the activity, mix several drops of food coloring with ¼ cup milk in small cups. Make a variety of colors for children to choose from. Ask children to wash their hands before doing the activity. Toast the bread for the children. Ask the children to paint a map on their piece of toast. Then children can use the knives to butter their toast and then munch their maps!

 ## Five Minute Social Studies Fun: I Know My Address!

- **Materials:** envelopes, pencils, paper, crayons or markers

Prior to this activity, ask each child to tell you his or her address. If a child has difficulty, write his or her address on a sheet of paper. Ask children to write their address on an envelope. Then ask children to write a short letter to or draw and color a picture for someone who lives with them. The children can put the letter or picture in the envelope, seal it, and "mail" it in their backpacks or school bags. Remind children at the end of the day to "deliver" their mail.

 ## Home Connection

Copy the Parent Letter on page 32 and send it home the week you are conducting this unit.

Date: _____

Dear Parents:

This week in social studies, we are learning about maps. We read the book *Me on the Map* by Joan Sweeney and talked about the purpose of maps and how to read them.

You can help your child learn more about maps by discussing them and looking at them at home. Here are some suggestions:

- Help your child find your country, your state, your town, and/ or your community on a map.

- Discuss the following questions with your child: What does a map show? What can you find on a map? Why do you think maps are important?

- Look at a globe with your child. If you do not have a globe at home, go to your local library. Discuss the different colors on the globe and what they represent.

According to the National Council for the Social Studies, "In the early grades, young learners draw upon immediate personal experiences as a basis for exploring geographic concepts and skills."

Thank you for being an important part of your child's learning.

Sincerely,

Name _____

I Can Read a Map!

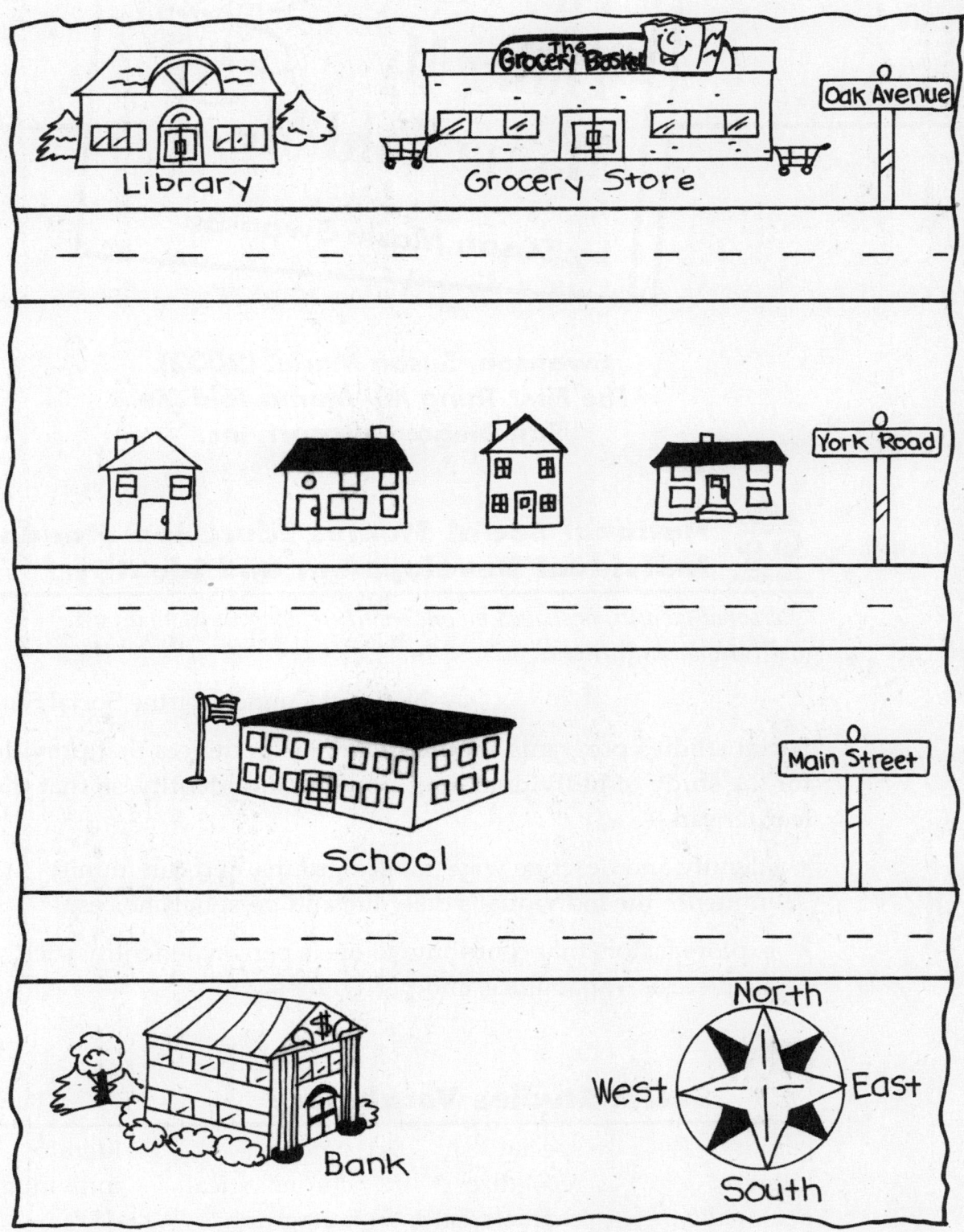

Rigby Best Teachers Press
Hey! There's Social Studies... SV 9781419034008

The First Thing My Mama Told Me

by Susan Marie Swanson

Swanson, Susan Marie. (2002).
The First Thing My Mama Told Me.
San Diego: Harcourt, Inc.

National Social Studies Education Standard: Individual Development and Identity

"Personal identity is shaped by one's culture, by groups, and by institutional influences."

—National Council for the Social Studies

Social studies programs should include experiences that provide for the study of individual development and identity, so that the learner can—

- identify and describe ways family, groups, and community influence the individual's daily life and personal choices.

- explore factors that contribute to one's personal identity such as interests, capabilities, and perceptions.

Social Studies Vocabulary

name	special	unique	identity
interest	recognize	chronological	individuality
personality	characteristics	autograph	

Hey! There's Social Studies... SV 9781419034008

Prereading Activity

- **Materials:** *The First Thing My Mama Told Me* by Susan Marie Swanson, paper, pencil

Conduct a picture walk through the book with the children. Make sure the children notice that this story is *chronological*, meaning it is told in the order of events. The story begins when the little girl is born and continues through her seventh birthday. Ask the children to predict what they think they might learn from reading this book. Record the children's suggestions on a sheet of paper.

Read-Aloud Activity

- **Materials:** *The First Thing My Mama Told Me* by Susan Marie Swanson, children's suggestions from the Prereading Activity above

Read *The First Thing My Mama Told Me* aloud with the children. Ask the children to *recognize* Lucy's *name* throughout the book. Revisit the children's suggestions from the Prereading Activity. Discuss the similarities and differences between the children's suggestions and what they actually learned from the story.

Application and Practice Activity

- **Materials:** one flashlight for every two or three children (You may want to ask parents to loan these.)

Turn out the lights in your classroom. Put children into groups of two or three. Provide each group with a flashlight. The children can take turns writing their names in the air with the flashlights, just as Lucy did in the story.

Extension Activity

- **Materials:** none needed

Discuss things that shape each person's identity, such as family, friends, interests, choices, and abilities. Invite each child to share a few interesting facts about themselves, such as the names of family members or friends, favorite sports or foods, and so on. Then play a game of "I'm Thinking Of" with the children. Start by saying "I'm thinking of a person who…" and complete the sentence with something unique about a particular child. The children can guess which child you are talking about.

Literacy Center Ideas

Reading/Writing: Letters in the Sand

- **Materials:** sand table or a sand/salt tray (shoe box lid with sand or coarse salt)

Ask each child to name someone in his or her family. Children can use a finger to write the family member's name in the sand or salt. Children can also write their own name or a friend's name if they choose.

Math: Counting Names

- **Materials:** several different varieties of math counters

The children can use math counters to spell their names. Then ask the children to count the number of math counters they used to spell their names. The children can repeat the activity with different types of counters and compare the number of counters used each time.

Hey! There's Social Studies… SV 9781419034008

Science: Finding Fingerprints

- **Materials:** paper, washable stamp pads, magnifying glasses

Have a class discussion on individual physical differences, such as hair and eye color, height, and right- and left-handedness. Explain that while some people may have certain *characteristics* in common, everyone has a *unique* set of fingerprints. The children can make fingerprints using a washable stamp pad and paper. Have the children use magnifying glasses to examine the fingerprints closely to see how they are different.

Social Studies: Similarities and Differences

- **Materials:** All About Me activity (page 40), All About Us activity (page 41), pencils

Make a copy of the All About Me activity and the All About Us activity for each child. The children will first complete the All About Me activity with information about themselves. Working in pairs, the children will then complete the All About Us activity. The children can use the Venn diagram to discuss similarities and differences between them and their partner.

Art: Life-Sized Me

- **Materials:** butcher block paper, crayons or markers, yarn, pieces of fabric, glue

Help the children trace each other's bodies on large sheets of butcher block paper. The children can use crayons or markers to color their creations and then add yarn for hair and fabric for clothing. You may want to display these "Life-Sized Me" pictures in the hallway.

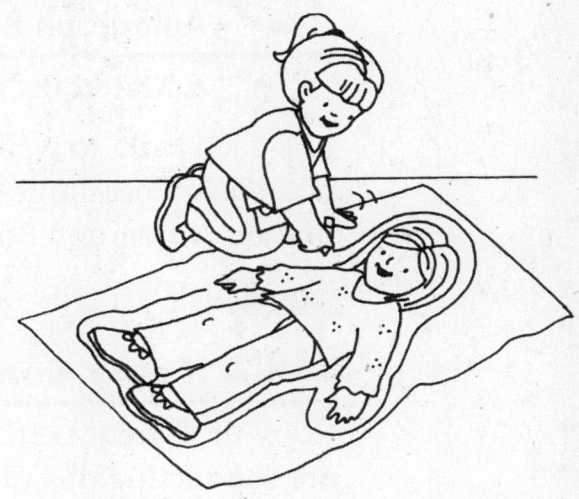

Hey! There's Social Studies... SV 9781419034008

Dramatic Play: Me Bags

- **Materials:** personal items from each child, a canvas or cloth bag, permanent or paint marker

Write the word *ME* on a canvas or cloth bag using a marker. Send home the Supply Request Letter on page 89 the week before doing the activity. Ask families to send personal items that represent their child's *personality*, *interests*, and *individuality*. The children can take turns putting their items in the ME bag to share.

Kids in the Kitchen: Edible Names

- **Materials:** stick pretzels, knotted pretzels, place mats

Caution: This activity uses edible items. Always check for food sensitivities and allergies before serving food or allowing children to handle food.

The children can use stick and knotted pretzels to spell their name on place mats. Demonstrate how to break off pieces of the pretzels and put them together to make curved or straight letters. Invite children to enjoy eating their name!

Five Minute Social Studies Fun: Autograph Book

- **Materials:** markers, one small spiral notebook per child

Ask each child to write his or her name in the front of a small spiral notebook. Encourage the children to get each classmate's autograph in their Autograph Book.

Home Connection

Copy the Parent Letter on page 39 and send it home the week you are conducting this unit.

Date:

Dear Parents:

This week in social studies, we are learning about individual development and identity. We read the book *The First Thing My Mama Told Me* by Susan Marie Swanson and talked about characteristics that are unique to each person, such as fingerprints. We made an autograph book, we shared Me Bags, and we investigated our fingerprints.

You can help your child learn more about individual development and identity by encouraging discussions at home. Here are some suggestions:

- Ask your child to talk about his or her favorite things, such as TV programs, games, sports, or foods. Share your favorite things as well and discuss the similarities and differences.

- Use a washable stamp pad to make fingerprints with your child. Use a magnifying glass to look closely at the fingerprints and compare and contrast them.

- Use stick pretzels and knotted pretzels to spell the names of your family members with your child. When you are finished, enjoy the "edible names" as a snack.

According to the National Council for the Social Studies, questions such as *How do people learn? Why do people behave as they do?* and *What influences how people learn, perceive, and grow?* are important to the study of how individuals develop from youth to adulthood.

The time you spend with your child is important. Thank you for your contributions.

Sincerely,

Name _____

All About Me

Directions: Fill in the blank in each sentence.

My age is _____ .

I am in _____ grade.

My eyes are the color _____ .

My hair is the color _____ .

I have _____ brother(s).

I have _____ sister(s).

I go to _____ School.

When I grow up, I want to be a(n) _____ .

My favorite animal is a(n) _____ .

My favorite food is _____ .

Rigby Best Teachers Press
Hey! There's Social Studies... SV 9781419034008

All About Us

Directions: Write details that tell how you are different in the outer circles. Write details that tell how you are alike where the circles overlap.

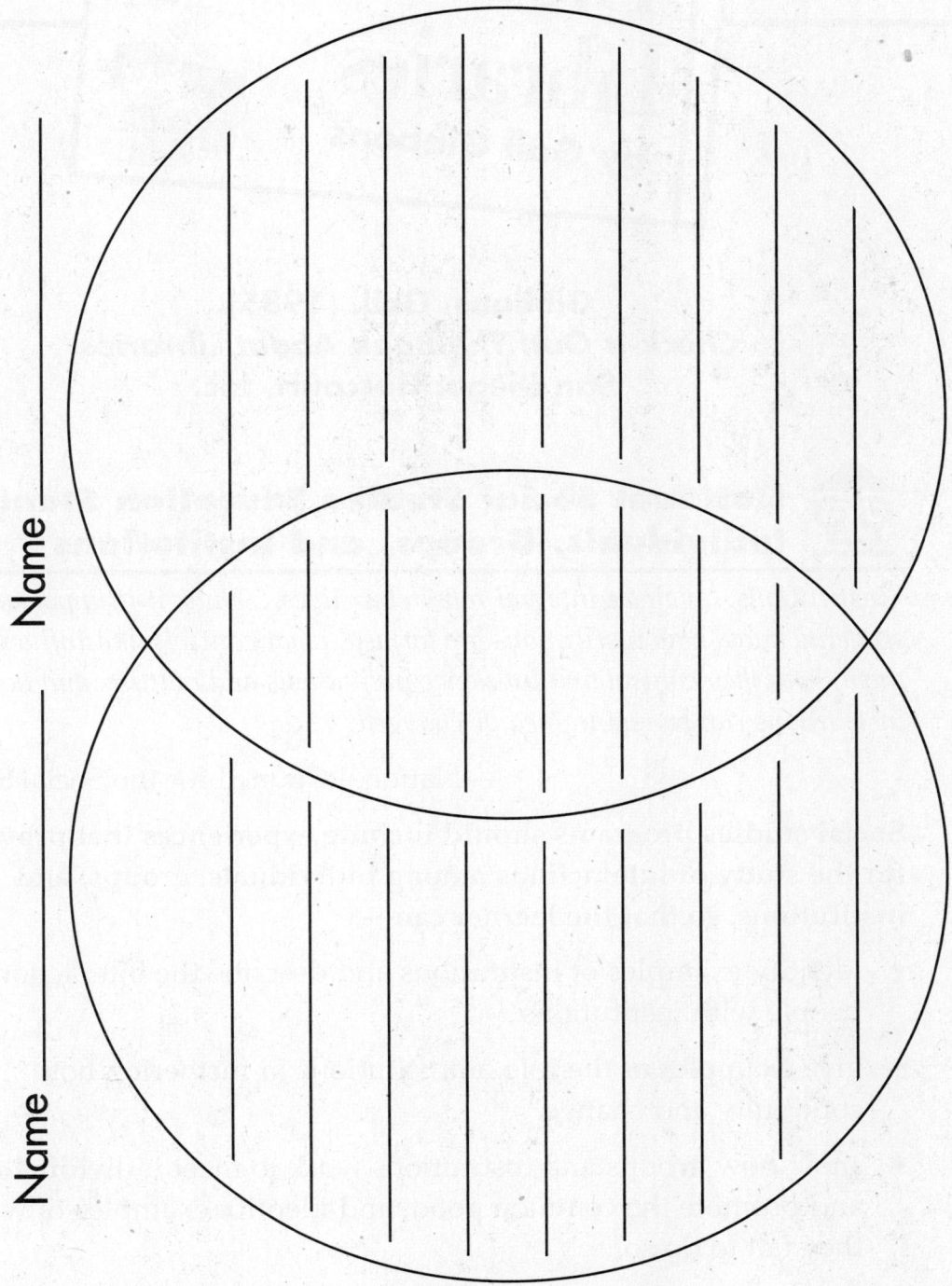

Name

Name

Rigby Best Teachers Press
Hey! There's Social Studies... SV 9781419034008

**Check It Out!
The Book About
Libraries**
by Gail Gibbons

**Gibbons, Gail. (1985).
Check It Out! The Book About Libraries.
San Diego: Harcourt, Inc.**

National Social Studies Education Standard: Individuals, Groups, and Institutions

"Institutions…play an integral role in our lives…Thus, it is important that students know how institutions are formed, what controls and influences them, how they control and influence individuals and culture, and how institutions can be maintained or changed."

—National Council for the Social Studies

Social studies programs should include experiences that provide for the study of interactions among individuals, groups, and institutions, so that the learner can—

- identify examples of institutions and describe the interactions of people with institutions.

- give examples of the role of institutions in furthering both continuity and change.

- show how groups and institutions work to meet individual needs and promote the common good, and identify examples of where they fail to do so.

 ## Social Studies Vocabulary

library	published	information	public
librarian	fine	date	call number

 ## Prereading Activity

- **Materials:** *Check It Out! The Book About Libraries* by Gail Gibbons, chart paper, marker, a library book

Ask children to tell what they know about libraries. If your school or community does not have a library with which children are familiar, discuss the benefits of a library. If children are familiar with libraries, ask them to discuss what they want to learn from reading this book. Record the children's suggestions on chart paper, making a KWL chart. The first column will be what the children **K**now about libraries, the second column will be what the children **W**ant to know about libraries, and the third column will be what the children **L**earned about libraries. Share the library book with the children. Point out such features as the bar code, due date, and library stamp, if applicable.

 ## Read-Aloud Activity

- **Materials:** *Check It Out! The Book About Libraries* by Gail Gibbons, the KWL chart from the Prereading Activity above, marker

Read *Check It Out! The Book About Libraries* aloud with the children. Ask the children to tell you what they learned from this story. Record their suggestions on the KWL chart in the third column. Revisit all columns on the chart with the children.

Application and Practice Activity

- **Materials:** none needed

Take the children to the school library, if you have one. If not, set up a classroom library. Allow the children to explore the materials in the library and to ask questions of the librarians. Remind the children of the story they read and what they learned.

Extension Activity

- **Materials:** none needed

If possible, take the children on a field trip to a local library. Allow them to explore the materials in the library and to ask questions of the librarians. Remind the children to follow library rules, such as talking quietly and not disturbing others.

Literacy Center Ideas

Reading/Writing: Thank-you Notes

- **Materials:** paper, pencils, chalkboard or dry erase board, chalk or dry erase marker

Prior to the activity, ask children to brainstorm a list of words they might want to use when writing a thank-you note to a librarian. Write the list on the board. Children can choose whether the note will be for the school librarian or a librarian in the community. Ask children to think about all of the things a librarian does to help people. The children can include examples of these things in their note. Encourage the children to write more than one note if they choose.

 **Math:** How Many Books?

> • **Materials:** classroom library books

Children can work in pairs for this activity. One child can stand while the other child stacks books to equal his or her partner's height. Then the children can work together to count the number of books in the stack.

 **Science:** Computer Science Search

> • **Materials:** an Internet-capable computer

If your local library has a Web site, show the children how to log on to that site. Demonstrate a search in the online catalog for science materials. If your local library does not have a Web site, demonstrate how to conduct a search on the Internet for science materials. Discuss the benefits of using computer technology to search quickly for materials.

 Social Studies: The Biggest Library

> • **Materials:** several nonfiction books about the Library of Congress

Allow the children to look through books about the Library of Congress. Encourage the children to find three facts they did not know and share one of the facts with the class.

 **Art:** At the Library Class Book

> • **Materials:** At the Library activity (page 49), pencils, crayons or markers

Make one copy of the At the Library activity for each child. The children will draw a picture of themselves at the library and complete the sentence at the bottom of the page. Compile these activity pages into a class book and allow each child to take turns taking the book home to share with his or her family.

Dramatic Play: Classroom Library

- **Materials:** books, index cards, small table and chair

The children can set up a classroom library in the dramatic play area. They can use a small table and chair as a librarian's desk. The children can pretend to check out books using index cards to write their name and the date.

Kids in the Kitchen: Bookworms

- **Materials:** three cherry tomatoes per child, toothpicks, raisins, low-fat cream cheese, plastic knives, one small paper plate per child

 _Caution:_ *This activity uses edible items. Always check for food sensitivities and allergies before serving food or allowing children to handle food.*

Ask children to wash their hands prior to the activity. The children will work on small paper plates. The children can use toothpicks to attach three tomatoes together, which will form a bookworm. Then the children can use the cream cheese to attach two raisins for eyes. After the bookworms are assembled, the children will enjoy eating them for a snack!

Five Minute Social Studies Fun: Library Poster

- **Materials:** one sheet of poster paper per child, crayons or markers

The children can make a poster that shows a benefit of the library, such as checking out books, working on a computer, or reading a newspaper. If your school has a library, you might want to display these posters near the entrance.

Home Connection

Copy the Parent Letter on page 48 and send it home the week you are conducting this unit.

A B C D E F G H I J K L M

Date:

Dear Parents:

This week in social studies we are learning about libraries. We read *Check It Out! The Book About Libraries* by Gail Gibbons and talked about the importance of libraries. We wrote a thank-you note to a librarian, and we learned about the biggest library in the United States, which is the Library of Congress.

You can help your child learn more about libraries by discussing them at home and visiting them often. Here are some suggestions:

- Take a weekly or monthly trip to a local library with your child. If possible, sign up to take a class together.

- Go to the library with your child and talk to a librarian about his or her job. Ask questions and take notes on what you've learned.

- If your child does not have a library card of his or her own, find out if you can obtain one at your local library. Discuss the responsibilities involved in owning a library card.

According to the National Council for the Social Studies, "Young children should be given opportunities to examine various institutions that affect their lives and influence their thinking."

Together we are sending your child on the road to academic success. Thank you for your participation.

Sincerely,

N O P Q R S T U V W X Y Z

48

At the Library

I can _____ at the library.

Rigby Best Teachers Press
Hey! There's Social Studies... SV 9781419034008

Name _____

The Trip Back Home

by Janet S. Wong

Wong, Janet S. (2000). *The Trip Back Home.*
San Diego: Harcourt, Inc.

National Social Studies Education Standard: Culture

"In a democratic and multicultural society, students need to understand multiple perspectives that derive from different cultural vantage points. This understanding will allow them to relate to people in our nation and throughout the world."

—National Council for the Social Studies

Social studies programs should include experiences that provide for the study of culture and cultural diversity, so that the learner can—

- describe ways in which language, stories, folktales, music, and artistic creations serve as expressions of culture and influence behavior of people living in a particular culture.

- give examples and describe the importance of cultural unity and diversity within and across groups.

- explore and describe similarities and differences in the ways groups, societies, and cultures address similar human needs and concerns.

Social Studies Vocabulary

| culture | diversity | family | travel |
| tradition | passport | pen pal | |

Prereading Activity

- **Materials:** *The Trip Back Home* by Janet S. Wong

Read aloud the title of the book and look at the cover with the children. Ask the children what they think this book might be about. Discuss visiting *family* and/or friends and what things the children might do to prepare for a trip.

Read-Aloud Activity

- **Materials:** *The Trip Back Home* by Janet S. Wong, a large world map

Read *The Trip Back Home* aloud with the children. Discuss with the children some of the Korean traditions and cultural elements that were in this story. Show the children where Korea is located on a world map. If any of the children are Korean, have Korean relatives, or have visited Korea, invite them to share their experiences with the class.

Application and Practice Activity

- **Materials:** none needed

To help the children appreciate differences in others, ask each child to share a family routine with the class. This routine can be for bedtime, a mealtime, a holiday, and so on. Explain to the children that each family does things its own way, and there isn't a right way or a wrong way.

Extension Activity

• **Materials:** an Internet-capable computer

Help children learn more about other cultures by introducing them to the concept of a *pen pal*. A good site to visit is http://www.epals.com/.

Literacy Center Ideas

Reading/Writing: The Trip Back Home

• **Materials:** paper, pencils

Have children imagine that they have moved away from home to another community. Ask them to write a short story about a trip back home to see their family. Children can include the names of family members, traditions, and activities in which they would participate.

Math: How Far?

• **Materials:** large, detailed map of the United States or the world, math counters

Spread the map out on the floor in the Math Center. Have children find the state or the country in which they live. Then have children choose another place that they might like to visit. The children can make a line of math counters from place to place and count how many math counters are in between the two.

www.harcourtschoolsupply.com

52

Rigby Best Teachers Press
Hey! There's Social Studies... SV 9781419034008

Science: Comparing and Contrasting Cultures

- **Materials:** Comparing and Contrasting Cultures activity (page 57), crayons

Make a copy of the Comparing and Contrasting Cultures activity for each child. The children can look at the pictures that represent scenes from the story. Then have children draw a picture of the way the same scene would be illustrated in their culture or another culture with which they are familiar. For example, there was a wood-burning stove in the story, and most families in the United States have electric or gas stoves.

Social Studies: Map It Out

- **Materials:** large bulletin board or chalkboard, large world map, several small self-stick notes for each child

One week prior to this activity, send the Supply Request Letter on page 89 home. Ask families to supply a list of places in the world in which they have relatives or friends. Families can also indicate places from which their ancestors came. Display the world map on a bulletin board or chalkboard. The children can look at the lists provided by their families and use self-stick notes to indicate the locations on the map. After all the children have had a turn, encourage them to look at the map and notice the locations of their families and friends.

Art: Korean Kite

- **Materials:** several different kinds of paper, including tissue and typing paper; sticks; straws; string; glue; markers

The traditional Korean kite is made with bamboo sticks and Korean paper. You can show the children some examples at http://www.csun.edu/~ghsiung/fighters4.html and http://www.gombergkites.com/. The children can use the papers, markers, sticks, straws, and strings to create a replica of a Korean kite. You can also find a list of materials and some simple directions at http://www.gombergkites.com/nkm/plan3.html.

Dramatic Play: Guess the Tradition

- **Materials:** none needed

Each child can think of a tradition that his or her family has, such as a holiday tradition, a bedtime routine, or a game. Then have each child dramatize the family tradition while the other children guess what is being portrayed.

Kids in the Kitchen: Children with Chopsticks

- **Materials:** one pair of wooden chopsticks per child (most Asian restaurants would be willing to donate them to a teacher); one paper bowl per child; a variety of food cut into cubes, such as cheese, fruit, and vegetables; rubber bands. (You may want to ask parents to donate the food items.)

 *Caution: This activity uses edible items. Always check for food sensitivities and allergies before serving food or allowing children to handle food.*

Ask children to wash their hands prior to the activity. The children may choose which foods they would like to sample and put them into a bowl. Then the children will try using the chopsticks to eat the food. If children are having trouble, put a rubber band around one end of the chopsticks to help keep them together.

Rigby Best Teachers Press
Hey! There's Social Studies... SV 9781419034008

Five Minute Social Studies Fun: Children's Day

- **Materials:** none needed

South Korea celebrates Family Month, with special days for parents, grandparents, and children. Tell children to imagine that they will be celebrating Children's Day. Have children suggest foods they would like to eat, activities or games in which they would like to participate, and music they would like to listen to on their special day.

Home Connection

Copy the Parent Letter on page 56 and send it home the week you are conducting this unit.

Date:

Dear Parents:

This week in social studies, we are learning about culture. We read the book *The Trip Back Home* by Janet S. Wong and talked about the importance of cultural traditions and cultural diversity. We ate with chopsticks, celebrated Children's Day, and made a Korean kite.

You can help your child learn more about cultural traditions and cultural diversity by exposing your child to different cultures. Here are some suggestions:

- Take your child to cultural events in your community, such as festivals, art fairs, and concerts.

- Go to the library with your child and check out books about cultures that are different from your own. Encourage your child to learn more about other cultures on the Internet.

- Find cultural recipes and try making some of them at home with your child.

According to the National Council for the Social Studies, "During the early years of school, the exploration of the concepts of likenesses and differences in school subjects such as language arts, mathematics, science, music, and art makes the study of culture appropriate."

Thank you for your cooperation.

Sincerely,

Rigby Best Teachers Press
Hey! There's Social Studies... SV 9781419034008

Name _____

Comparing and Contrasting Cultures

Rigby Best Teachers Press
Hey! There's Social Studies... SV 9781419034008

Worksong

by Gary Paulsen

Paulsen, Gary. (1997). *Worksong.*
San Diego: Harcourt, Inc.

National Social Studies Education Standard: Production, Distribution, and Consumption

"People have wants that often exceed the limited resources available to them. As a result, a variety of ways have been invented to decide upon answers to four fundamental questions: What is to be produced? How is production to be organized? How are goods and services to be distributed? What is the most effective allocation of the factors of production (land, labor, capital, and management)?"

—National Council for the Social Studies

Social studies programs should include experiences that provide for the study of how people organize for the production, distribution, and consumption of goods and services, so that the learner can—

- describe how we depend upon workers with specialized jobs and the ways in which they contribute to the production and exchange of goods and services.

- give examples of the various institutions that make up economic systems, such as families, workers, banks, labor unions, government agencies, small businesses, and large corporations.

Social Studies Vocabulary

goods   services   workers   jobs   tools

Prereading Activity

- **Materials:** *Worksong* by Gary Paulsen, chart paper, marker

Discuss with children that *goods* are things *workers* make or grow for people who need or want them. Tell children that *services* are things people do for others. On a chart, write two headings, "Goods" and "Services." Ask children to brainstorm a list of goods and services. Record their suggestions on the chart. Explain that the story you are going to read today is about people who work to provide goods and services for others.

Read-Aloud Activity

- **Materials:** *Worksong* by Gary Paulsen

Read the book *Worksong* aloud with the children. Discuss the illustrations on each page. Ask the children to tell what each person is doing on each page, and whether that person is providing a good or a service.

Application and Practice Activity

- **Materials:** chart paper, markers

Ask children to think about who works at school. Discuss what *jobs* the people do and what *tools* they might use. On a chart, write two headings, "Job" and "Tools." Record children's responses on the chart. Make sure the chart includes principals, teachers in various grades and subjects, librarians, custodians, secretaries, or other personnel in your school.

Job	Tools
custodian	broom
librarian	computer

Extension Activity

- **Materials:** chart paper, marker

Ask the children to talk about the names of various professions. For example, a person who makes or repairs shoes is called a shoemaker, and a person who draws plans for buildings is called an architect. Discuss other professions that children suggest and record these suggestions on chart paper.

Literacy Center Ideas

Reading/Writing: Chef for a Day

- **Materials:** recipes or cookbooks, paper, pencils

Tell children that one of the jobs of a chef is to create recipes. Often, chefs write down their recipes to share with others. Allow children to look through recipes or cookbooks for reference. Ask children to draw a picture of a favorite food at the top of their paper. If children are able, ask them to write the name of the food as well. Then ask children to dictate how the food is made as you write the recipe. You may want to bind these recipes into a class cookbook.

mac and cheese

1. Put some macaroni in a pan on the stove.
2. Add some cheese.

Math: What Would You Buy?

- **Materials:** play money, catalogs and sale flyers of interest to the children, paper, pencils

Prior to the activity, give each child a set amount of play money, such as $10.00. Allow the children to look through the catalogs and sale flyers. Ask the children to make a list of items they would like to purchase if they had real money. Remind the children to keep track of their "purchases" on a sheet of paper so they can track their spending.

Science: Scientific Careers

- **Materials:** paper, pencils, crayons or markers, nonfiction books about science and scientific careers

Ask the children to think of careers in the field of science. Provide some nonfiction books about science and scientific careers in the science center. Then ask the children to draw a picture of themselves doing some work in a scientific field. You may want to compile these drawings into a class book to display in the science center.

Social Studies: Goods or Services?

- **Materials:** Goods and Services activity (page 64), pencils

Make a copy of the Goods and Services activity for each child. The children can look at each picture and indicate whether it represents a good or a service by circling the correct word.

Art: Artist for a Day

- **Materials:** construction paper; several different types of art media, such as paint, crayons, markers, colored pencils, chalk, and so on

Tell the children that they will be artists for the day. The children can choose different types of media to use on construction paper. Encourage the children to try using different techniques as well. You may want to display their creations in the classroom.

Dramatic Play: Wonderful Workers

- **Materials:** various clothing and tools that might be used by community workers, such as a firefighter's hat, a police badge, a nurse's uniform, a doctor bag, a mail carrier bag, and so on

Children can dress up like a community worker and dramatize doing that job. They can pretend to be part of a community of workers.

61

Rigby Best Teachers Press
Hey! There's Social Studies... SV 9781419034008

 ## Kids in the Kitchen: My Own Recipe

- **Materials:** a variety of fruits cut into bite-sized pieces, such as apples, oranges, bananas, strawberries, and grapes; one small paper bowl per child; plastic spoons; index cards; pencils

 *Caution: This activity uses edible items. Always check for food sensitivities and allergies before serving food or allowing children to handle food.*

Ask children to wash their hands prior to the activity. The children can make their own recipe by choosing which ingredients they want to add to their bowl. As the children add each ingredient, they can make a list of the ingredients on an index card. When the children have finished making their "recipes," they can write the name of the recipe at the top of the card and enjoy their creation!

 ## Five Minute Social Studies Fun: Would You Rather?

- **Materials:** none needed

The children can play a game of "Would You Rather?" Each child can take a turn asking another child a question such as "Would you rather provide a good or a service?", "Would you rather work in an ice cream shop or in a factory?", or "Would you rather be a chef or a firefighter?" Encourage the children to ask questions about the working world.

 ## Home Connection

Copy the Parent Letter on page 63 and send it home the week you are conducting this unit.

Hey! There's Social Studies... SV 9781419034008

Date:

Dear Parents:

This week in social studies, we are learning about the production and exchange of goods and services. We read the book *Worksong* by Gary Paulsen and talked about the importance of people who provide goods and services. We pretended to be chefs, artists, and scientists, and we played a game.

You can help your child learn more about goods and services by discussing them on a daily basis. Here are some suggestions:

- When you run errands with your child, ask him or her to name five goods and five services that are being provided at the places you visit.

- Ask your child to write a thank-you note to someone who provides a good or a service for your family.

- Discuss your profession with your child and ask your child if you are providing a good or a service.

According to the National Council for the Social Studies, "Young learners…explore economic decisions as they compare their own economic experiences with those of others and consider the wider consequences of those decisions on groups, communities, the nation, and beyond."

When you turn everyday events into teachable moments, the impact is very powerful. Thank you for your cooperation.

Sincerely,

Goods and Services

good service	good service	good service
good service	good service	good service
good service	good service	good service

Rigby Best Teachers Press
Hey! There's Social Studies... SV 9781419034008

The Computer
by Gayle Worland

Worland, Gayle. (2004).
The Computer. (Fact Finders: Great Inventions.)
Mankato, MN: Capstone Press.

National Social Studies Education Standard: Science, Technology, and Society

"Modern life as we know it would be impossible without technology and the science that supports it."

—National Council for the Social Studies

Social studies programs should include experiences that provide for the study of relationships among science, technology, and society, so that the learner can—

- identify and describe examples in which science and technology have changed the lives of people, such as in homemaking, childcare, work, transportation, and communication.

Social Studies Vocabulary

computer	technology	communication	abacus
transportation	calculator	mouse	laptop
CD-ROM	Internet	device	keyboard

Hey! There's Social Studies... SV 9781419034008

Prereading Activity

- **Materials:** *The Computer* by Gayle Worland, chalkboard or dry erase board, chalk or dry erase marker

Look at the cover of the book with the children. Ask the children if they think this is a current book or an older book and why they think so. Discuss how the computer on the cover looks as compared to how a computer of today looks. Have the children predict what they might learn about *technology* from reading this book. Write their suggestions on the board.

Read-Aloud Activity

- **Materials:** *The Computer* by Gayle Worland

Read *The Computer* aloud with the children. Discuss the photos on each page. After reading the book, ask the children to share what they learned about technology. Write their suggestions on the board near their predictions from the Prereading Activity above. Ask the children to compare their predictions with what they actually learned from reading the story.

Application and Practice Activity

- **Materials:** several nonfiction books and/or photos that depict the history of computers

Allow children to look through nonfiction books and photos that depict the history of computers. Show some of the photos together and ask the children to name some similarities and differences among the different types of computers. Discuss inventions such as the *mouse*, the *laptop*, and the *CD-ROM* and ask children to think about how these inventions have improved technology.

Hey! There's Social Studies... SV 9781419034008

Extension Activity

- **Materials:** an Internet-capable computer

Invite children to think of a topic that they wish to know more about. As each child shares his or her topic, help the child type it into an Internet search such as http://yahooligans.yahoo.com/. Demonstrate to the children how easy it is to search for information using the Internet.

Literacy Center Ideas

Reading/Writing: Time for Kids

- **Materials:** an Internet-capable computer

Help children log on to http://www.timeforkids.com/TFK/ on the Internet. Ask the children to read about something on this site and share one thing they learned with their classmates.

Math: Problem Solving

- **Materials:** paper, pencil, an abacus (if available), a calculator, a computer

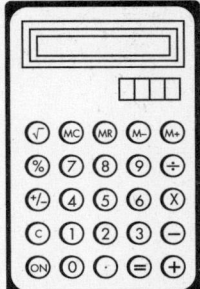

Ask volunteers to compute a two-digit addition problem. One child will solve the problem using paper and pencil, one child will use an *abacus* (if available), one child will use a *calculator*, and one child will use a computer. Ask the children to discuss which method was the fastest, the slowest, the easiest, and the most difficult. Explain that while a computer provides a faster way to obtain information, it may not be the fastest way to compute a math problem. The children will probably find that using the calculator was the fastest way to solve the problem. Explain that a calculator is another example of technology.

 **Science:** Talk to Me!

- **Materials:** paper, pencils

Tell the children that they are going to get the chance to be inventors. Talk about the many devices that people use to communicate, such as telephones, computers, and walkie-talkies. Discuss the features of each *device* and how they are used. Guide children to discuss their opinions about which devices they like best and why they think the devices work well. Then invite each child to invent a new communication device and make a sketch of it. Encourage children to be as imaginative as possible and think of other fun things their communication devices could do. For example, a new device could be the scooter phone. You can ride it while talking on it.

 **Social Studies:** Technology and Inventions

- **Materials:** an Internet-capable computer, paper, pencil

Help children log on to http://www.factmonster.com/homework/ hwscience-scitech.html#tech to view different types of technological inventions and discuss how they have changed people's lives. Children can make a list of five inventions they don't think they could live without.

 **Art:** Crayola.com

- **Materials:** an Internet-capable computer, a printer, paper

Allow the children to visit http://www.crayola.com/ and create a work of art. If possible, allow the children to print their creations to take home or display in the classroom.

Dramatic Play: No Technology?

- **Materials:** none needed

The children can pretend that they live in a world without technology. Remind them that everyday items such as TVs, telephones, refrigerators, and digital clocks would not have been invented without technology. The children can discuss what life in a world without technology would be like. Ask them which inventions they would have liked to help create.

Kids in the Kitchen: Keyboard Crunch

- **Materials:** one graham cracker per child, low-fat cream cheese, plastic knives, alphabet letter cereal, one small paper cup per child, one place mat per child

 *Caution: The activity uses edible items. Always check for food sensitivities and allergies before serving food or allowing children to handle food.*

Ask children to wash their hands prior to the activity. Children should work on place mats for this activity. Give each child a graham cracker, a plastic knife, and a small paper cup of alphabet letter cereal. Children can spread cream cheese on the graham cracker and put the alphabet letter cereal on the cracker to represent the letters of a computer *keyboard*. They may put the letters in the same or a different order if they choose. Then children can enjoy eating their crunchy snack!

Hey! There's Social Studies... SV 9781419034008

 **Five Minute Social Studies Fun:** Survey Says

- **Materials:** paper, pencils

The children can take a survey of how many computers are in homes today. If possible, take the children on a walking trip through the school. Remind them to be quiet in the hallways so as not to disturb others. The children can make a quick stop in each classroom as well as the office and ask for a show of hands to represent people who have at least one computer in their home. Help the children tally their numbers to find a total.

 **Home Connection**

Copy the Parent Letter on page 71 and send it home the week you are conducting this unit.

Date:

Dear Parents:

This week in social studies, we are learning about technology. We read the book *The Computer* by Gayle Worland and talked about the history of technology. We found several fun Web sites for kids and made a crunchy snack.

You can help your child learn more about technology at home. Here are some suggestions:

- If you have a personal computer at home, go on the Internet with your child and search for fun children's Web sites. If you do not have a computer at home, go to your local library and use a computer there.

- Help your child take apart an old calculator (or purchase an inexpensive one for this purpose). Discuss what you see inside.

- Discuss with your child how communication and technology have changed over the years.

According to the National Council for the Social Studies, "Young children can learn how technologies form systems and how their daily lives are intertwined with a host of technologies. They can study how basic technologies such as ships, automobiles, and airplanes have evolved and how we have employed technology such as air conditioning, dams, and irrigation to modify our physical environment."

Thank you for contributing to your child's scientific understanding.

Sincerely,

A River Ran Wild

by Lynne Cherry

**Cherry, Lynne. (1992). *A River Ran Wild*.
San Diego: Harcourt, Inc.**

National Social Studies Education Standard:
Global Connections

"The realities of global interdependence require understanding the increasingly important and diverse global connections among world societies."

—National Council for the Social Studies

Social studies programs should include experiences that provide for the study of global connections and interdependence, so that the learner can—

• explore causes, consequences, and possible solutions to persistent, contemporary, and emerging global issues, such as pollution and endangered species.

• give examples of conflict, cooperation, and interdependence among individuals, groups, and nations.

• examine the relationships and tensions between personal wants and needs and various global concerns, such as use of imported oil, land use, and environmental protection.

 ## Social Studies Vocabulary

reduce	reuse	recycle	conserve
pollution	cause	solution	prevention
resources	receptacles	trash	pollutant

 ## Prereading Activity

- **Materials:** *A River Ran Wild* by Lynne Cherry

Conduct a class discussion about things children can do to *reduce, reuse,* and *recycle resources.* Explain to children that *pollution* exists in the air, on land, and in water. If we work together to reduce, reuse, and recycle, we can help decrease pollution. Ask children to draw a picture of how they can do their part, for example, turning off the faucet while brushing their teeth. Look at the cover of the book *A River Ran Wild* with the children and discuss the illustrations.

 ## Read-Aloud Activity

- **Materials:** *A River Ran Wild* by Lynne Cherry

Read the book *A River Ran Wild* aloud with the children. Discuss the illustrations on each page. Pause after each page and discuss the text. Ask questions such as, "Why do you think the Nashua people loved their land so much?", "Why do you think the settlers decided to build along the river?", and "Why did the river become polluted?" Encourage children to share their experiences with pollution.

Application and Practice Activity

- **Materials:** Responsibility for Our Resources activity (page 80), pencils, crayons or markers

Make a copy of the Responsibility for Our Resources activity for each child. Discuss some things people can do each day to help decrease pollution, such as recycle a can, reduce the amount of water used, or reuse paper. Ask children to complete the activity by writing about or drawing a picture of something they will do or have already done today to take responsibility for our resources.

Extension Activity

- **Materials:** 2–3 pretzels or small crackers per child

 *Caution: This activity uses edible items. Always check for food sensitivities and allergies before serving food or allowing children to handle food.*

Give each child a few pretzels or small crackers. Encourage them to eat all of the food items. When the food is eaten and gone, introduce the word *consume* and talk about how the food is like the earth's resources. When they are all used up, or consumed, we can't bring them back—no matter how much we want or need to.

www.harcourtschoolsupply.com

74

Rigby Best Teachers Press
Hey! There's Social Studies... SV 9781419034008

Literacy Center Ideas

Reading/Writing: Conserving Water

- **Materials:** paper, pencils, crayons

The children can write and/or draw about ways in which they can conserve, or save, water. These ways might include turning off the faucet when brushing their teeth, washing dishes by hand instead of using a dishwasher, or taking a bath instead of a shower.

Math: Water Pollution Graph

- **Materials:** small math counters in a variety of colors, one small plastic zipper bag for every three to four children, chart paper, markers

Prior to the activity, put a small number of math counters in a variety of colors into a plastic zipper bag for each group of three to four children. Discuss the meaning of the word *pollutant* with children and tell them that the math counters are going to represent different kinds of pollutants. The bag represents a water sample. Make a graph on chart paper to show how much of each pollutant is in the "water sample." Invite children to count the number of math counters in their bags by color and use markers to record the data on the chart. Discuss ways in which to keep water clean and free from pollutants.

 Hey! There's Social Studies... SV 9781419034008

GLOBAL CONNECTIONS

 **Science:** A Substitute for Juice Boxes?

- **Materials:** one empty juice box, one pair of scissors, one small sheet of paper, one dropper, one small paper cup of water for every pair of children, newspaper

Prior to the activity, cover the work area with newspaper. The children will make observations of a juice box. Have them cut the juice box in half using the scissors. Ask children to think about what materials the juice box is made from. Have children put a drop of water on the sheet of paper. Then have them put a drop of water on the outside of the juice box. Discuss what happened. Ask them to decide if they think a juice box would be easy to recycle. Children can name other containers from which to drink juice that would be environmentally better for the earth.

 **Social Studies:** We Love Garbage!

- **Materials:** various clean, empty containers such as oatmeal containers, shoe boxes, yogurt containers; construction paper; tape; glue or paste; crayons or markers; scissors; decorative materials such as glitter, ribbon, yarn, and beads

Discuss with the children that one way to stop littering might be to make beautiful *trash receptacles*. Have small groups choose a container they would like to decorate. Children can also make a label with the words "We Love Garbage!" or "My Car Trash Box" to place on their receptacles.

Hey! There's Social Studies... SV 9781419034008

 ## Art: Recycled Sculpture

- **Materials:** items that can be recycled, such as plastic milk cartons or jugs, lids, cardboard boxes, and so on (You may want to ask parents to donate these items.)

The children can use items that can be recycled to create a sculpture. Discuss the importance of reusing and recycling objects to help keep the earth clean.

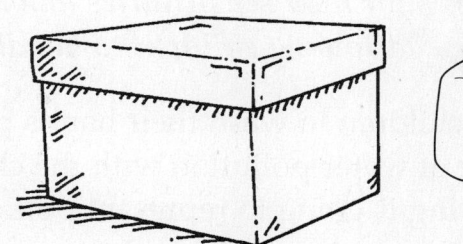

 ## Dramatic Play: Pretend Pollution

- **Materials:** none needed

The children can pretend that they live near a river that has a lot of pollution. They can pretend to be a person, plant, or animal affected by the pollution and discuss ways to prevent it.

 ## Kids in the Kitchen: "Polluted" Shake

- **Materials:** food coloring, milk, large plastic container with seal-tight lid, one small paper cup per child

 *Caution: This activity uses edible items. Always check for food sensitivities and allergies before serving food or allowing children to handle food.*

Ask children to wash their hands prior to the activity. Revisit the topic of water pollution with the children. Tell them that the food coloring is going to represent pollution and the milk is going to represent a river, lake, or ocean. Pour some milk into the container. Each child can take a turn adding one drop of food coloring to the milk. After all children have had a turn, seal the container tightly and give it a gentle shake. The milk will turn a very dark color. Pour into glasses for each child to taste if they choose.

 ## Five Minute Social Studies
Fun: Litter Walk

- **Materials:** garbage bags, plastic gloves for each child

Weather permitting, take the children on a short "Litter Walk" near the school. The children can count how many pieces of litter they collect and take pride in keeping their community clean.

 ## Home Connection

Copy the Parent Letter on page 79 and send it home the week you are conducting this unit.

Hey! There's Social Studies... SV 9781419034008

Date:

Dear Parents:

This week in social studies, we are learning about pollution. We read the book *A River Ran Wild* by Lynne Cherry and talked about the importance of keeping the earth clean. We went on a "Litter Walk" to help clean up our community, and we made a "Polluted" Shake!

You can help your child learn more about pollution by modeling ways to help. Here are some suggestions:

- If your family does not recycle, find out about recycling programs in your community. If your family does recycle, find out about other recycling programs that are available in your community.

- Take a "Litter Walk" with your child. Bring a large garbage bag and some rubber gloves so you can safely pick up and discard litter in your area.

- Make a "3 Rs Chart" at home. Ask family members to document how they **R**educe, **R**euse, and/or **R**ecycle on a daily basis.

According to the National Council for the Social Studies, "Through exposure to various media and first-hand experiences, young learners become aware of and are affected by events on a global scale. Within this context, students in early grades examine and explore global connections and basic issues and concerns, suggesting and initiating responsive action plans."

Thank you for your participation.

Sincerely,

Rigby Best Teachers Press
Hey! There's Social Studies... SV 9781419034008

Name _____

Responsibility for Our Resources

Today I

(circle one or more)   recycled   reduced the amount used   reused

(item) _____ .

Rigby Best Teachers Press
Hey! There's Social Studies... SV 9781419034008

Good Citizenship Counts
by Marie Bender

Bender, Marie. (2003). *Good Citizenship Counts*. Edina, MN: ABDO Publishing Company.

National Social Studies Education Standard: Civic Ideals and Practices

"An understanding of civic ideals and practices and citizenship is critical to full participation in society and is a central purpose of the social studies."

—National Council for the Social Studies

Social studies programs should include experiences that provide for the study of the ideals, principles, and practices of citizenship in a democratic republic, so that the learner can—

- identify examples of rights and responsibilities of citizens.

- recognize and interpret how the "common good" can be strengthened through various forms of citizen action.

Social Studies Vocabulary

respect	caring	responsibility	fairness
honesty	courage	citizen	character
volunteer	rights	rules	laws
helping			

Prereading Activity

• **Materials:** *Good Citizenship Counts* by Marie Bender

Read the title of the book with the children. Discuss the meaning of the word *citizen*. Ask children to talk about the photo on the front of the book. What are the children doing in this picture? How are they showing good citizenship? Ask the children to name some things they could do that would show good citizenship.

Read-Aloud Activity

• **Materials:** *Good Citizenship Counts* by Marie Bender

Explain to the children that good citizens make careful decisions and they learn to solve problems. Citizens are people who live in a community, city, state, or country. They have certain *rights* and *responsibilities*. As you read the story with the children, discuss the photos on each page.

Application and Practice Activity

• **Materials:** Hector Helps activity (page 88), scissors, two envelopes per child, pencils

Make a copy of the Hector Helps activity for each child. Discuss with the children that there are different kinds of *helping*. Sometimes people help others and sometimes they help themselves. Help children write "Helping Others" on one envelope and "Helping Myself" on the other envelope. Ask children to cut the pictures apart on the activity page and sort them into the appropriate envelopes. For example, the picture of Hector making a sandwich would go into the envelope labeled "Helping Myself."

Extension Activity

- **Materials:** stuffed animals

Send home the Supply Request Letter on page 89 a few days before doing this activity. Ask families to send one favorite stuffed animal to school with each child. Discuss the importance of responsibility with the children. Ask children to describe responsibilities they have at home and at school. Tell children that they are going to be responsible for keeping their stuffed animals with them throughout the day. Just before the end of the day, gather the children together to discuss their responsibilities in *caring* for their stuffed animals.

Literacy Center Ideas

Reading/Writing: Respectfulness

- **Materials:** chalkboard or dry erase board, chalk or dry erase marker, index cards, pencils, crayons or markers

Invite the children to play a game about *respect*. First ask children to brainstorm a list of actions that show respect. For example, "A girl says please when asking for something." Record the list on the chalkboard or dry erase board. Then ask children to list other actions that do not have anything to do with respect, such as, "A boy walks home." Have children write one action on each index card. Ask them to add a smiley face to the actions that show respect. Save these cards for the Five Minute Social Studies Fun activity on page 86.

 **Math:** Small-Group Sorting

- **Materials:** several containers, a variety of math manipulatives

Prior to the activity, fill several containers with a variety of math manipulatives, such as counters, pattern blocks, or marbles. Have children work together in small groups to sort manipulatives according to color, size, shape, or other attributes.

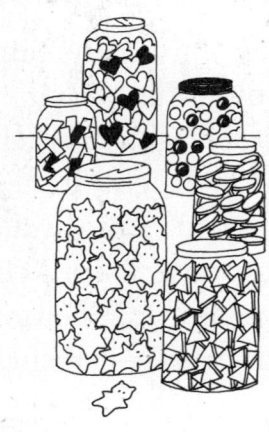

 **Science:** Responsible Recycling

- **Materials:** several clean, empty containers, some items that are recyclable and some items that are non-recyclable (You may want to ask parents to donate these items.)

Have children discuss the rules for recycling in their community. Then ask children to sort the containers into two groups: recyclable and non-recyclable.

 **Social Studies:** Excellent Expectations

- **Materials:** poster board, markers

Discuss with children the importance of rules and expectations. Good citizens follow the *rules* and *laws* of their communities. Ask children to brainstorm a list of expectations for their classroom. Record children's suggestions on the poster board and hang it in the classroom as a daily reminder.

Art: Citizen Cutouts

- **Materials:** People Patterns (page 26), scissors, crayons or markers, glue or paste, craft sticks

Prior to the activity, make several copies of the People Patterns for each student. Discuss people in the community who show good citizenship, such as volunteers. Have children use crayons or markers to draw features on the patterns, creating people who show good citizenship. Then ask children to cut out the patterns and glue them to craft sticks. The children can use these puppets in the dramatic play area.

Dramatic Play: The Talk with Me Table

- **Materials:** a small table and a few chairs, puppets from the Art activity above

Put a small table and a few chairs in the dramatic play area. When children have an issue that requires discussion, encourage them to go to the "Talk with Me Table" and talk it out with the people involved. This can help reduce the amount of tattling that goes on in your classroom, as well as demonstrate the importance of talking over problems. Invite children to use the puppets they created in the Art activity above as someone to talk to.

 ## Kids in the Kitchen: Taking Turns Treat

- **Materials:** dried fruit pieces, pretzels, various types of cereal, large bowl, measuring cups, plastic gloves

 *Caution: This activity uses edible items. Always check for food sensitivities and allergies before serving food or allowing children to handle food.*

Ask children to wash their hands prior to the activity. Discuss with children the importance of taking turns. Explain that *fairness* is part of being a good citizen. Ask each child to measure ¼ cup of an ingredient and empty it into the large bowl. Put on the plastic gloves and mix the ingredients together. Children will enjoy the snack that they worked together to create.

 ## Five Minute Social Studies Fun: R-E-S-P-E-C-T

- **Materials:** index cards from the Reading/Writing activity on page 83

Collect all of the index cards from the Reading/Writing activity on page 83 and shuffle them together. Tell children that you are going to read the sentences that they wrote. Children should respond by giving three short claps when they hear a card that tells about respect and by not clapping at all if the card does not tell about respect.

 ## Home Connection

Copy the Parent Letter on page 87 and send it home the week you are conducting this unit.

Date:

Dear Parents:

This week in social studies, we are learning about being good citizens. We read the book *Good Citizenship Counts* by Marie Bender and talked about citizenship. We learned about responsibility, respectfulness, and working together. We played a game called R-E-S-P-E-C-T, and we made puppets.

You can help your child learn about being a good citizen by modeling good citizenship at home. Here are some suggestions:

- Talk about the word *responsibility* and what it means. Help your child identify various ways members of your family act responsibly.

- Have your child think of a task that he or she can perform regularly at home.

- Ask your child to think of something he or she can do to act in a more caring way toward someone, such as showing patience with a younger sibling or not interrupting when someone else is talking.

According to the National Council for the Social Studies, "In the early grades, students are introduced to civic ideals and practices through activities such as helping to set classroom expectations, examining experiences in relation to ideals, and determining how to balance the needs of individuals and the group."

Thank you for your participation.

Sincerely,

Rigby Best Teachers Press
Hey! There's Social Studies... SV 9781419034008

Hector Helps

A B C D E F G H I J K L M

Date: _____

Dear _____,

Thank you for offering to contribute materials for our classroom.

Please send the materials to school with your child in a labeled

plastic bag by _____.

This week, we are in need of the following:

_____

_____

_____

_____

_____

Thank you,

N O P Q R S T U V W X Y Z

Rigby Best Teachers Press
Hey! There's Social Studies... SV 9781419034008

Suggested Social Studies Vocabulary List

abacus
adopted
autograph
bodies of water
brother
calculator
call number
caring
cause
CD-ROM
character
characteristics
chronological
citizen
communication
computer
conserve
country
courage
culture
date
device
differences
diversity
divorced

fairness
family
father
fine
goods
grandfather
grandmother
helping
holiday
honesty
identity
individuality
information
interest
Internet
jobs
keyboard
landmarks
laptop
laws
librarian
library
map
married
mother

mouse
name
nationality
passport
pen pal
personality
pollutant
pollution
prevention
public
published
receptacles
recognize
recycle
reduce
resources
respect
responsibility
reuse
rights
rules
services
similarities
sister
solution

special
state
stepfather
stepmother
street
technology
tools
town
tradition
transportation
trash
travel
unique
volunteer
world
workers

Rigby Best Teachers Press
Hey! There's Social Studies... SV 9781419034008

Suggested Social Studies Literature List

CULTURE

Hoobler, Dorothy and Thomas. (1994). *The Mexican American Family Album*. New York: Oxford University Press.

Raven, Margot Theis. (2004). *Circle Unbroken*. New York: Farrar, Straus & Giroux (BYR).

Strickland, Dorothy S. and Michael R., eds. (1994). *Families: Poems Celebrating the African American Experience*. Honesdale, PA: Wordsong, Boyds Mills Press.

Wong, Janet S. (2000). *The Trip Back Home*. San Diego: Harcourt, Inc.

Wong, Janet S. (2002). *Apple Pie 4th of July*. San Diego: Harcourt, Inc.

INDIVIDUAL DEVELOPMENT AND IDENTITY

Jenness, Aylette. (1990). *Families: A Celebration of Diversity, Commitment, and Love*. Boston: Houghton Mifflin.

Kroll, Virginia. (1994). *Beginnings: How Families Come to Be*. Morton Grove, IL: Albert Whitman.

Leedy, Loreen. (1995). *Who's Who in My Family?* New York: Holiday House.

Pellegrini, Nina. (1991). *Families Are Different*. New York: Holiday House.

Super, Gretchen. (1991). *What Is a Family?* Frederick, MD: Twenty-First Century Books.

Super, Gretchen. (1991). *What Kind of Family Do You Have?* Frederick, MD: Twenty-First Century Books.

Swanson, Susan Marie. (2002). *The First Thing My Mama Told Me*. San Diego: Harcourt, Inc.

PEOPLE, PLACES, AND ENVIRONMENTS

Fanelli, Sara. (1995). *My Map Book*. New York: HarperCollins.

Hennessy, B. G. (2004). *The Once Upon a Time Map Book*. Cambridge, MA: Candlewick Press.

Knowlton, Jack. (1986). *Maps and Globes. (Reading Rainbow Book)*. New York: HarperTrophy.

Rabe, Tish. (2002). *There's a Map on My Lap! All About Maps*. New York: Random House.

Sweeney, Joan. (1996). *Me on the Map*. New York: Crown Publishers, Inc.

INDIVIDUALS, GROUPS, AND INSTITUTIONS

Gibbons, Gail. (1985). *Check It Out! The Book About Libraries*. San Diego: Harcourt, Inc.

Stewart, Sarah. (2001). *The Library*. New York: Farrar, Straus & Giroux.

Williams, Suzanne. (2002). *Library Lil*. New York: Penguin Young Readers Group.

Wing, Natasha. (2005). *The Night Before First Grade*. New York: Grosset & Dunlap.

Suggested Social Studies Literature List

PRODUCTION, DISTRIBUTION, AND CONSUMPTION

Dorros, Arthur. (2005). *Julio's Magic*. New York: HarperCollins.

Levin, Amy. (2003). *Hard Workers: Set C*. Minneapolis, MN: Compass Point Books.

Paulsen, Gary. (1997). *Worksong*. San Diego: Harcourt, Inc.

SCIENCE, TECHNOLOGY, AND SOCIETY

Adler, David A. (1995). *Calculator Riddles*. New York: Holiday House.

Cole, Joanna. (1999). *The Magic School Bus Gets Programmed*. New York: Scholastic.

Steinhauser, Peggy. (1997). *Mousetracks: A Kid's Computer Idea Book*. Berkeley, CA: Tricycle Press.

Worland, Gayle. (2004). *The Computer. (Fact Finders: Great Inventions.)* Mankato, MN: Capstone Press.

GLOBAL CONNECTIONS

Cherry, Lynne. (1992). *A River Ran Wild*. San Diego: Harcourt, Inc.

Cherry, Lynne. (2000). *The Great Kapok Tree: A Tale of the Amazon Rain Forest*. New York: Voyager Books.

Dr. Seuss. (1971). *The Lorax*. New York: Random House Books for Young Readers.

Peet, Bill. (1981). *The Wump World*. Boston: Houghton Mifflin.

CIVIC IDEALS AND PRACTICES

Bender, Marie. (2003). *Good Citizenship Counts*. Edina, MN: ABDO Publishing Company.

Clack, Barbara. (2005). *The Pledge of Allegiance*. Albany, TX: Bright Sky Press.

Pellegrino, Marjorie White. (1999). *My Grandma's the Mayor: A Story for Children About Community Spirit and Pride*. Washington, DC: Magination Press.

St. George, Judith. (2004). *So You Want to Be President?* New York: Philomel.

Suggested Social Studies Manipulative List

aprons

blocks

boats

cars

cash register

CD player

compass

disposable cameras

doctor bags

firefighter hats

flags from different nations

globes

lab coats

mail carrier bags or bins

maps

miniature multicultural people or dolls

miniature street signs

mirrors

multicultural music instruments

name badges

nurse uniforms

planes

police badges

puppets

puzzles

stop sign

tape recorder

toy animals

traffic light

trains

trucks

Rigby Best Teachers Press
Hey! There's Social Studies... SV 9781419034008

**Reading/Writing
Center**

**Math
Center**

**Science
Center**

**Art
Center**

**Dramatic Play
Center**

**Kids in the
Kitchen Center**

Social Studies Center

Rigby Best Teachers Press
Hey! There's Social Studies... SV 9781419034008

Web Sites

Harcourt Achieve Inc. is not responsible for the content of any Web site listed in this book except its own. All material contained on these sites is the responsibility of the hosts and creators. The Web site addresses are current as of the date of publication.

SOCIAL STUDIES STANDARDS
http://www.socialstudies.org/standards/strands/
http://cnets.iste.org/currstands/index.html

CULTURE
http://www.4children.org/news/9-97mlit.htm
http://funsocialstudies.learninghaven.com/links/world_cultures.htm
http://www.pbs.org/americaresponds/anationofcultures.html
http://pbskids.org/arthur/parentsteachers/activities/acts/culture_commotion.html
http://pbskids.org/clifford/parentsteachers/activities/have_respect/04_have_respect.html

PEOPLE, PLACES, AND ENVIRONMENTS
http://funsocialstudies.learninghaven.com/links/maps.htm
http://www.plcmc.org/forkids/mow/
http://www.maps.com/FunFacts.aspx?nav=FF

INDIVIDUAL DEVELOPMENT AND IDENTITY
http://pbskids.org/wayback/family/tp.html
http://pbskids.org/barney/pareduc/educators/lesson718.html
http://pbskids.org/readingrainbow/family/activities/activity89.html

INDIVIDUALS, GROUPS, AND INSTITUTIONS
http://www.publiclibraries.com/
http://lists.webjunction.org/libweb/

PRODUCTION, DISTRIBUTION, AND CONSUMPTION
http://www.bbc.co.uk/cbbc/yourlife/
http://www.bls.gov/k12/

SCIENCE, TECHNOLOGY, AND SOCIETY
http://web.mit.edu/invent/www/ima/
http://www.tekmom.com/students/

GLOBAL CONNECTIONS
http://www.pca.state.mn.us/kids/
http://www.epa.gov/kids/index.htm
http://www.oregonzoo.org/ConservationResearch/whatyou.htm
http://www.earthforce.org/
http://www.dnr.state.wi.us/org/caer/ce/eek/

CIVIC IDEALS AND PRACTICES
http://bensguide.gpo.gov/3-5/citizenship/responsibilities.html
http://www.hud.gov/kids/

Rigby Best Teachers Press
Hey! There's Social Studies... SV 9781419034008

Professional Resources

Alleman, J., & J. Brophy. (2001). *Social Studies Excursions, K–3—Book One: Powerful Units on Food, Clothing, and Shelter.* Portsmouth, NH: Heinemann.

Alleman, J., & J. Brophy. (2002). *Social Studies Excursions, K–3—Book Two: Powerful Units on Communication, Transportation, and Family Living.* Portsmouth, NH: Heinemann.

Alleman, J., & J. Brophy. (2003). *Social Studies Excursions, K–3—Book Three: Powerful Units on Childhood, Money, and Government.* Portsmouth, NH: Heinemann.

Baratta-Lorton, M. (1972). *Workjobs: Activity-centered Learning for Early Childhood Education.* Menlo Park, CA: Addison-Wesley.

Bredekamp, S., & C. Copple, eds. (1997). *Developmentally Appropriate Practice in Early Childhood Programs.* Rev. ed. Washington, DC: NAEYC.

Cerbus, Deborah P. (1992). *Connecting Social Studies and Literature.* Huntington Beach, CA: Teacher Created Materials.

Edwards, Barbara. (2001). *Using Multicultural Literature to Teach K–4 Social Studies: A Thematic Unit Approach.* Boston: Allyn & Bacon.

Fredericks, Anthony. (1991). *Social Studies Through Children's Literature: An Integrated Approach.* Portsmouth, NH: Teacher Ideas Press.

Fredericks, Anthony. (2000). *More Social Studies Through Children's Literature: An Integrated Approach.* Portsmouth, NH: Teacher Ideas Press.

Hilke, Eileen V. (1999). *Children's Literature and the K–4 Social Studies Standards.* Bloomington, IN: Phi Delta Kappa Educational Foundation.

Houser, Neil O. (1999). "Critical Literature for the Social Studies: Challenges and Opportunities for the Elementary Classroom." *Social Education*, 63(4), 212–215.

Laughlin, Mildred Knight, and Patricia Payne Kardaleff. (1991). *Literature-based Social Studies: Children's Books and Activities to Enrich the K–5 Curriculum.* Phoenix, AZ: Oryx Press.

McGowan, Thomas M., Lynnette Erickson, and Judith A. Neufeld. "With Reason and Rhetoric: Building the Case for the Literature-Social Studies Connection." *Social Education*, 60(4), 203–207.

Mindes, Gayle. "Social Studies in Today's Early Childhood Curricula." *Young Children: Beyond the Journal* (September 2005).

NCSS (National Council for the Social Studies). (2001). In Search of a Scope and Sequence for Social Studies. *Social Education*, 48(4), 376–85.

NCSS. (1994). *Curriculum Standards for Social Studies: Expectations for Excellence.* Washington, DC: NCSS.

Norton, D. E. (1985). "Language and Cognitive Development Through Multicultural Literature." *Childhood Education*, 62, No. 2, 103–108.

Readence, J. E., D. W. Moore, and R. J. Rickelman. (2000). *Prereading Activities for Content Area Reading and Learning.* Delaware: International Reading Association.

Roberts, Patricia L., and Nancy Lee Cecil. (1993). *Developing Multicultural Awareness Through Children's Literature: A Guide for Teachers and Librarians, Grades K–8.* Jefferson, NC: McFarland & Co.

Van Tine, Elizabeth, Shirley Lee, Camille Cooper, and Barbara White. (1999). *Super Social Studies! Quick and Easy Activities, Games, and Manipulatives.* New York: Scholastic.

Welton, David A. (2004). *Children and Their World: Strategies for Teaching Social Studies.* Boston: Houghton Mifflin.